Social Insecurities

Library of Congress Catalogue card number 89-51193
I S B N number 0-939775-05-0

Published by West Hill Press, Fitzwilliam NH 03447
Printed in U.S.A.

SOCIAL INSECURITIES

Written and Illustrated by
ROSALIND WELCHER

Published by

WEST HILL PRESS   NEW HAMPSHIRE

So I said to him, " *Harry, you only think of me as a sex object!*"

I ran into Marvin the other day. He's had a triple by-pass, a hair transplant and he just divorced his wife and married his secretary.

Judy (that's Marcia's oldest girl) has a new young man. They're sharing an apartment as long as their commitment lasts or until the lease expires...whichever comes first.

. . . . . now that Bill and I have finally agreed to separate, Mother, I feel that I need a little time to find myself and explore my potential, so I know you won't mind if Stacy and Meghan come to stay with you and Dad for a little while until-----

I just saw an add for a wonderful book, Herbie! It's called " Sex After Sixty," and it's set in large type!

It always gets my blood boiling when some young snip of a nurse one third my age calls me by my first name.

Sometimes I wonder if achieving a good body image is worth all the effort.

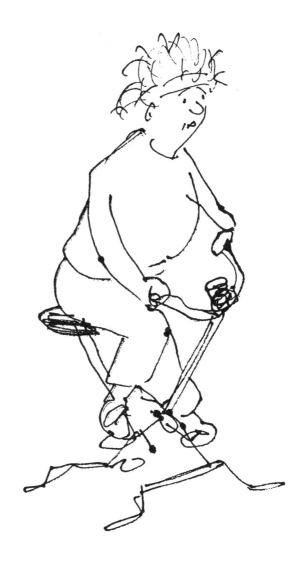

I was sitting next to Jim Tompkins while we were eating lunch at the Friendly Meals Center, and guess what! He patted my fanny! I guess that anti-wrinkle cream must be working!

Now that my barber retired I just can't get used to having my hair cut by some young girl in a beauty parlor.

Just when I complete the course at Madame Poisson's Ecole de Patisserie Francaise, the doctor goes and puts Herman on a low fat diet!

Mildred is getting married again. It's so romantic! It was a case of love at first sight! She met him at the clinic when they were both going to get their blood pressure tested.

I don't know whether I should let my hair go gray like Barbara Bush or make it blonde like Nancy Reagan.

I don't know what's gotten into my wife lately. She's always going around the house mumbling that I ought to get a hearing aid!

I always used to think that by the time I got to be this old someone would have invented a cure for old age.

You know, Janet, I'm glad I missed the sexual revolution. When I think of how much I used to hate just having to kiss some of my dates at the end of an evening ....

*Let's see . . . Monday we get our pressure
checked, Tuesday it's square dancing at the
golden Age Club. . . . . . Wednesday I get my eyes
examined, Thursday you pick up the new battery
for your hearing aid . . Friday we go to a lecture
on latest changes in Medicare, Saturday it's
Bingo at the V.F.W. . . . . My! It is a full week
ahead!*

I just bought this sport jacket, and when the salesman said it would last me a lifetime it suddenly hit me. He was probably right.

*When Jerry came out of the closet it took his father
and me a little while to get used to the idea, but now
he wants to bring his friend to our anniversary party,
and I don't know how Cousin Margaret and Uncle
Arthur will react, and my sister's husband is deathly
afraid of getting aids, and . . . .*

Why is it that when somebody like Jane Fonda does aerobics people say she's agile, but when I do the very same things they call me spry!

Sometimes I look around and I ask myself is this what I worked all those years for....so I can play golf three times a week and stay up late at night watching dirty movies on TV?

I ran into Helen in the supermarket and I told her we're going to Hawaii on a tour this summer, and she said she and Joe went there last fall . . .

and I said last fall we went to Rio, and she said they went to Rio the year before that . . .

and I said last march we went on a cruise to the Virgin Islands, and she said they cruised there three years ago . .

and then somehow I accidently dropped a can of peaches on her foot.

Now this isn't going to hurt a bit!

She says it's an old family recipe, but I know for a fact that Betty Crocker . . .

*Harriet is sure she's going to get aids! She was
bitten by a mosquito while she was getting her
hair done, and she's positive that Georgio (he's
her hairdresser) is gay!*

Let's see, I have to renew Marvin's blood pressure medicine and his anti cholesterol pills and my arthritis medicine and get some more calcium tablets and some vitamins E and C and some more antacid pills, and then I guess I'll stop at the liquor store and pick up a bottle of gin.

I'm all confused. It seems that just because I don't like something it doesn't necessarily mean it's good!

Oh, Doris, I just got some terrible news! It seems I'm allergic to oat bran!

Somebody really should tell Marian that she doesn't have legs like Betty Grable anymore.

Eddie and I belong to the Big Band generation too.

*Then I read that the latest research shows that
alcohol lowers your cholesterol . . .*

My God, Mabel, this is almost as bad as when I tried to teach you to drive a car thirty years ago!

Every time I say I wish I could get a face lift you say you like me the way I am, but I notice that whenever a good looking girl goes by you sure give her the once over!

*I was all set to move into Ebb Tide Estates when
they told me I couldn't take Muffy with me!*

Antiques! Why we had one of those in our kitchen when I was a kid!

I'd like to meet some nice man, Ruth, but I just can't bring myself to go to one of those singles bars.

Ever since George retired I've been after him to get a hobby, so what does he do? He takes up cooking! You know, Mabel, everybody always praised my potroast and my cheesecake to say nothing of my apple tart, but now all I do in the kitchen is clean up after the master chef!

Oh, Hilda, I feel so awful! The girl at the check-out counter gave me the senior citizen's discount without my having to ask for it!

We have just been handed an additional cancellation. Due to icy road conditions the bake sale of the Friends Of The Chesterton Library . . .

So when Julia said she wants to have her father come and stay with us now that he's getting too old to live by himself anymore I said sure before I remembered how I couldn't stand the old SOB before he moved to Florida.

*So what I say to you , Mrs. America, out there is GET
IN TOUCH WITH YOUR SEXUALITY!*

I just don't enjoy the holidays anymore. Joe has to watch his cholesterol. Mabel is on a salt free diet. Helen and Jim are vegetarians, and Thelma won't let the twins eat anything made with sugar.

I exercise for fifteen minutes every morning, and I meditate for ten minutes every afternoon, and I try not to bottle up my hostilities, and I've learned to like yogurt, but I still don't feel good about myself!

I just came from Harry's funeral. He was run over by a car while he was jogging to the health food store.

David is bringing Debbie and Michael (they're from his marriage to Judy), and Helen (she's the girl he's living with) is bringing her three from her second marriage or whatever, and Marcia and Ted are bringing . . .

Well, Arthur, my brother Bill always says, "Never trust anyone under 55!"

This is my husband. He's a notch baby!

You know, Alice, I never thought volunteer work would be dangerous, but yesterday when I brought old Mr. Mulligan his Meal On Wheels he chased me all over the room in his wheelchair yelling " Give us a kiss, sweetiepie !"

It was such a lovely Christmas! We got a card from Mark and Judy in Cleveland, and Jason called us from San Diego . . . . and Lizzie wired us from Paris, and Arthur and Joannie sent us a tape from Phoenix. It was like having the whole family together again!

I told Louise I want to sell the house and buy a boat and sail to Tahiti. She says I'm having a late life crisis.

It's pretty discouraging. All the men our age want younger women, and the older ones are all look-ing for a nurse.

Well, I guess I'm going to be a grandmother at last. Joanie says her biological clock is running down, so she's going to get herself artificially inseminated.

. . . . so I said to him, but Herbert, we've been married thirty nine years, and she's young enough to be your daughter, and he said well I'm sorry, Dorothy, but we only go around once you know . . . .

I just don't see why they can't make movies any-more without all those dirty words in them!

You read all these stories about older women having romances with younger men, but where do you find these younger men?

My, Dr.Buxler, I bet you do a wonderful Lindy!

We try to live right.
Gladys takes a calcium
supplement, and I take
an aspirin every other
day . . .

. . . and Gladys uses
that new anti wrinkle
cream, and I'm using
that stuff that's sup-
posed to restore your
hair . . .

. . . and we both eat
lots of fiber, and Gla-
dys uses one of those
stationary bikes, and I
have a rowing
machine . . .

and we both try to
avoid cholesterol, and
we're taking a course in
stress management
and biofeedback....

......and then I
just read that
the most important
thing is how long your
grandparents lived!

Roy is in traction. He was wearing his new bifocals, and when he stepped onto the down escalator . . . .

My nightmare is that I'll drop dead and my daughter in law will come and go through my closets!

I'm thinking of going on a cruise. I hear an unattached guy like me has to fight off the women with a club!

Getting old may not be a barrel of laughs, but it sure beats the alternative.